DECIPHERING YOUR DREAMS

Reveal the mysteries of the world of dreams!

Written by Léa Schalk

Translated by Ciaran Traynor

Health and Wellbeing   50MINUTES.com

DECIPHERING YOUR DREAMS

- **Problem**: have you ever woken up with a start after a nightmare, with no idea where it came from? Or had a strange dream where intriguing, meaningless elements were all mixed together? But why do we dream? What role do our dreams play? And can we really find out what they mean?
- **Aims**: understand how dreams work and how they influence our daily lives, and discover how to interpret them.
- **FAQs:**
  - Does everyone dream?
  - Do we constantly dream when we are asleep?
  - What is the point of dreams?
  - Why do I not always remember my dreams?
  - What are precognitive dreams? Do they really exist?
  - Can dreams influence my everyday life?
  - How can I interpret my dreams by myself?

There is nothing more intimate and personalised than dreaming. A dream is a sort of nocturnal film, where we are both the director and the protagonist, more often than not without us even being aware of it. However, it cannot be denied that the frantic pace of our everyday lives means that they are usually the least of our worries. Few people take the time to examine their unlikely imaginary adventures when they wake up. But who among us has never woken up in a panic, or even in tears, after a nightmare, overwhelmed by terrifying thoughts? "Was it a dream? Why did I dream that?" And, on the other hand, who has never tried to make a sweet dream last longer, to see where it would take them? Our dreams call out to us, all the more so when they are strange or distressing.

Are dreams nothing more than meaningless fantasies or, on the contrary, are they valuable sources of information on our subconscious? How much attention should we pay to them? Why do they often leave nothing more but faint memories? Is it possible to remember them better, or even understand them? What does the science say? These are all questions that we will attempt to answer in this guide, while keeping our eyes wide open.

WHERE DO DREAMS COME FROM?

SLEEP CYCLES AND THEIR PHASES

Understanding our dreams and their psychological dimension is a fascinating topic, but what is going on from a purely physiological point when we dream? Certain branches of contemporary clinical neuroscience– meaning the medical specialities which study the nervous system, such as neurology and sleep medicine – focus on the direct study of brain activity in order to better understand several questions, including the phenomenon of dreams.

At the end of the 1950s, the French researcher Michel Jouvet noticed an unexpected phenomenon with the help of an electroencephalogram. He called it paradoxical sleep (most commonly known today as rapid eye movement sleep), a stage of sleeping which is now associated with dreaming. Jouvet describes it as paradoxical because of the contrast between extreme eye movement and brain activity with a listless, often difficult-to-wake body.

DID YOU KNOW?

Rapid eye movement sleep is not only a human phenomenon. In fact, it has been proven that all warm-blooded animals, including birds and other mammals, go through the same sleep phase.

In order to better understand the phases of rapid eye movement sleep – and therefore the time when we dream, according to several experts – during a night's sleep, it is helpful to know they are made up of a succession of cycles of around 90 to 120 minutes long. During a typical night's sleep, the average person will go through three to five of these cycles, during which scientists distinguish several phases:

- **Slow-wave sleep**, which lasts between 60 and 75 minutes and is made up of four stages:
    - Drowsy sleep is a state of semiconsciousness, during which the sleeper is easily woken up (stage 1).
    - Light sleep is the phase we go through most often during the night. It represents around 50% of our sleep time (stage 2).
    - Deep sleep makes up the third and fourth stages. During the first part of this phrase, muscular energy and brain activity decrease, after which we reach the deepest level of slow-wave sleep.
- **Paradoxical sleep** (REM, or rapid eye movement sleep), which lasts between 10 and 20 minutes. During this period, the brain is a hive of activity, sometimes even using more oxygen than when we are trying to solve a complex problem.
- **Intermediary sleep**, which is a very short period of semi-wakefulness between the different cycles.

From the moment we get under the covers, we normally need no more than 20 minutes to sink into a deep, slow-wave sleep. During this transition, there is a change in the electric waves emitted by our brains, which progressively slow, making us less and less receptive to external stimuli, unless these stimuli are very loud or considered important by the sleeper (saying their name, crying, etc.). Deep slow-wave sleep, which allows us to fully recover from our day, is more pronounced during the first half of the night, which is the reason why these first few hours of sleep are extremely restful. Moreover, there is a certain amount of brain activity, linked to simple and decontextualized sensory impressions (for example, feelings of coldness and heat, or emotions such as sadness, fear, and so on). It is rare for sleepers who are woken up during this period to remember their dreams in detail. However, this stage of our nightly journey is any-thing but a long, quiet river. After this period of slow-wave sleep, brainwaves accelerate and the hypnogram – a graph which allows you to visualise the different stages of sleep and awakening – begins to show intense brain activity: we are in full REM sleep. There is a large amount of complex dream activity, with a storyline, characters, powerful sen-sorial impressions, and so on. If the sleeper wakes up or is woken up by someone during this phase, they will be able to remember their dream in great detail and with considerable accuracy. This phase of intense nervous activity represents about 20% of an adult's sleep time, 40 to 50% of a child's, and even more in unborn children.

DID YOU KNOW?

Since your muscles are sluggish and your body immo-bile during REM sleep, it is not unusual to feel that you are paralysed during a dream.

Once you have got through the turbulent phase of REM sleep, you move into intermediary sleep, during which you again become sensitive to external stimuli. If you are not woken up at this point, another cycle will start, and this short period of wakefulness will quickly be forgotten. In the morning, going through a micro-awakening at the end of a cycle could naturally cause you to wake up completely.

WHY DO WE DREAM?

What role do our dreams play?

We spend around one third of our lives asleep. According to several specialists who have established a direct link between REM sleep and dreaming, dreams make up almost 20% of the time we spend sleeping. Consequently, a 50-year-old man, for example, will have spent more than three years of his life dreaming. Although some experts believe it is impossible to quantify the amount of time we spend dreaming every night, it is now certain that normal physiological sleep (meaning that the sleeper is not ill or taking medication) always involves dreaming.

Bu what role do dreams play exactly? Why do we dream? We still have a long way to go before we find the answer to that question. There are many different theories, with some even going as far to refute the existence of the link between dream activity and REM sleep.

According to the Nobel Prize winner Francis Crick and his colleague Graeme Mitchison, the main function of REM sleep is to sort all the information we accumulate during the day and erase the least pertinent, in order to avoid overloading the brain. However, this theory does not seem to be based on irrefutable scientific evidence.

According to other recent research in neurobiology, dreams summarise our thoughts from the day in order to allow us to better assimilate them and make wiser decisions – and therefore be more efficient – the following day. It perfectly illustrates the age-old saying "it's best to sleep on it".

For others, dreams encourage brain creativity, ensure emotional regulation and, during a child's development, even help young minds to discover or perfect certain abilities. Did you know that babies smile, and make other facial expressions, for the first time during REM sleep? Another theory sees dreaming as an adaptive trait to deal with stress. Indeed, it has been noted that when we are stressed or hurt, the length of REM sleep increases, as if our minds are trying to find a solution to isolate and protect themselves from physical stress and pain. These are all fascinating hypotheses, but they have never been proven.

What about nightmares?

We still know relatively little about this particular sort of dream, which often brings you out in a cold sweat. It was not until the mid-2000s that Tore Nielsen, a psychologist at the Hôpital du Sacré-Cœur de Montréal, the director of the Dream and Nightmare Laboratory and a pioneer in the subject, created the first model of how nightmares work. In his opinion, they are not necessarily a sign of some inner malaise; on the contrary, they are actually a way to master our fears, to make them tolerable and to allow us to digest certain difficult episodes of our lives. If the nightmare does what it is supposed to, we will sleep on peacefully. However, if it fails, then we wake up with a start, trembling in fear of our anxieties and our doubts. There are therefore good and bad nightmares. Bad nightmares can even become pathological if they recur frequently, haunt you during the daytime and cause insomnia, out of fear of having to relive these unpleasant episodes. This type of nightmare is often observed in those who have lived through some sort of trauma, such as war, assault, natural disasters, and so on.

DECIPHERING YOUR DREAMS

FROM ONEIROMANCY TO PSYCHOANALYSIS

Due to their seemingly elusive, mysterious nature, dreams have intrigued man since the dawn of time. History abounds with almost legendary stories of dreams which influenced the course of events. There are a number of historical figures whose exploits or misadventures were guided by dreams – from Constantine the Great (Roman Emperor, born sometime between 270 and 288 and died in 337) to Charlemagne (King of the Franks, 742/747-814), not to mention Joan of Arc (French heroine, 1412-1431) and Abraham Lincoln (16th President of the United States, 1809-1865).

DID YOU KNOW?

The American inventor Elias Howe (1819-1867) would probably have never completed his sewing machine if he had not dreamt that he was being taken to be executed by warriors holding spears that were pierced near the head.

Even though the psychological phenomenon of dreaming has been observed throughout history, it has not always been viewed as it is now. In civilisations such as those in Egypt, Ancient Greece or Ancient Rome, dream incubation and interpretation were common practices. In other words, dreams had an important role in society, to such an extent that both the Greeks and the Egyptians built sleep temples, where it was believed that certain illnesses could be cured. To this end, patients would sleep on the ground and wait for a divinity to appear to them in a dream. They would then ask them questions about their health, the cause of their illness and the treatment to apply. In certain temples, special priests would even help their disciples to correctly interpret their dreams.

Far from being a recent fad, the search for the key to our dreams can be traced back to the ancient past. There are even accounts of dream analysis transmitted through Egyptian papyrus. However, it was not until the 2nd century AD under the Roman Empire that the first work dedicated to oneiromancy, or divination based on dreams, was released. In his *Oneirocritica*, Artemidorus Daldianus (Greek writer, 2nd century AD) classified dreams into five different categories. However, although it was seen as reliable at the time, the book is now of no objective use.

The interpretation of dreams was also important for these ancient civilisations because dreams represented a privileged opportunity to meet with the gods. As they were an expression of divine will, they therefore had to allow the will of the gods to be carried out. In the works of Homer, for example, dreams are associated with the immateriality of the dead and their souls, through which the divinity expresses their message to the sleeper.

After being dismissed for several centuries as nothing more than superstition, dreams returned to the limelight with the birth of psychoanalysis. Sigmund Freud (Austrian neurologist, 1856-1939) described dreams as "the royal road to the unconscious" and believed that they could cure emotional problems if their significance could be understood. However, he approached the question in a completely different manner than in ancient times: while dreams were considered to be divine messages in the past, Freud's theory involves buried childhood desires, particularly sexual ones. In other words, there were no more prophetic messages and divine visits at night: for Freud, a dream was a puzzle which came straight from inside.

Later, Carl Gustav Jung (Swiss psychiatrist and psychoanalyst, 1875-1961), a wayward follower of Freud, introduced the notion of collective unconscious, a sort of compilation of archetypical images which are common to the whole of humanity, and which therefore fundamentally refers to the same thing for everyone. Unlike Freud's theory, sexuality does not play a defining role for Jung. The Swiss scientist sees dreams primarily as a way to re-establish an individual's psychological balance by reconnecting their conscious and unconscious identity.

Today, psychoanalysis continues to emphasise the importance of this intimate research, which brings wisdom and inner strength. The only way to go about this is, of course, to analyse the content of your dreams.

ANALYSING YOUR DREAMS WITH THE HELP OF MENTAL HEALTH PROFESSIONALS

Is there a place for the study of the content of dreams, including nightmares, in medical science? Can it be used as a therapeutic tool to treat physical and psychological problems?

From a medical point of view, searching for meaning in our dreams based on some absolute frame of reference has no place in the 21st century. Indeed, as Dr Daniel Neu, a sleep specialist and neuro-psychologist at the Brugman University Hospital in Brussels, argues, there is merit to analysing dreams as long as the person's individual situation is taken into account. In particular, the use of the content of dreams has its place when, for example, recurring nightmares are symptomatic of serious mental or psychological problems, such as post-traumatic stress disorder.

Does this apply to you? Good news: with the help of a psychotherapist, you can now finish the nightly work certain nightmares failed to do through Image Rehearsal Therapy (IRT). This technique, which has already proven effective, involves helping the victim of nightmares to reclaim their negative dream memories in order to overcome them. In more concrete terms, the psychotherapist will invite you to visualise your bad dream for the first time by closing your eyes. They then move on to the re-writing step: you have to make the scenario into something positive and repeat it in your head for five to ten minutes every day. It has been proven that this newly constructed story is very likely to come up in a dream. According to Canadian studies, an adult needs two to three weeks to carry out this task, but it has an 80% success rate!

However, apart from very distressing cases like nightmares, remembering your dreams has little use as far as sleep medicine is concerned, which considers that the benefits of remembering them has never been proven. Moreover, according too much importance to dreams is not only unnecessary, but could also become upsetting or even dangerous. Psychoanalysis, on the other hand, takes a completely different look at the question of the therapeutic value of dreams.

TEST: SHOULD I CONSULT A SLEEP SPECIALIST?

Do any of these points sound familiar?

- I often struggle to fall asleep, and sometimes I am even afraid to do so.
- I talk in my sleep.
- I regularly suffer from sleep apnoea.
- I involuntary grind my teeth when I sleep.
- I sleepwalk.
- I suffer from night terrors. I make panicked cries but no one can wake me up.
- I move when I dream and I can become violent without meaning to.
- I do sexual things while I am asleep.
- I sometimes suddenly fall asleep during the day, irrespective of the time.
- I regularly have frightening or upsetting nightmares.

If any of these statements applies to you, you should think about consulting a sleep specialist, who will be able to give you a proper diagnosis.

Therefore, with the exception of certain cases, the study of dreams is not part of the field of neuroscience. Indeed, since the meaning of dreams is so elusive and varies from one person to another, it is too removed from scientific objectivity. If you feel that there is a message in your dreams, you should go to a psychoanalysist or a psychotherapist, many of whom see the interpretation of dreams as a potential goldmine of information on the individual in general. The aim of this can be to work on what is bothering them or just to allow them to get to know themselves better.

> "I use to have a rather mechanical sex life; what mattered for me was being able to perform in bed. But at some point I realised that that wasn't enough any more; I was constantly frustrated and unhappy. I wanted to have a more sensual sex life, but I felt incapable of letting myself go with a woman. I often had worrying, incomprehensible dreams where I would do disgusting things with animals, which always ended very badly. I decided to consult a specialist, who helped me to analyse my dreams and find out what they meant. I realised what was holding me back in my love life and it reassured me. Today, I feel that I'm completely in control of my sex life." (François, 30)

In François' case, interpreting his dreams with the help of a psychoanalyst helped him to reconstruct certain obstacles and difficulties and finally liberate himself from this burden. According to certain specialists, analysing your dreams can help you reach this awareness far more quickly. There are also signal dreams, which can help you to find solutions to your problems. Did you know, for example, that just beginning psychotherapy can stimulate the dreams that you are trying to understand and which hold the answers you are looking for? Obviously, the most difficult thing to do is to then interpret them correctly. Inès Carels, a Belgian psychologist, says that the best way for professionals to understand others' dreams is to first take the time to understand their own.

Pierre Daco, an internationally renowned Belgian psychologist and psychoanalyst, argues that dreaming is as essential for our mental and psychological balance as food and sleep, and defines it as a sort of "psychological breathing"[1] (2013). The majority of the characters in our dreams are nothing more than aspects of ourselves, which is yet another reason to take a serious interest in oneirology.

On a broader note, Aude Jullien, a psychologist, sexologist and oneirologist based in Brussels, claims that taking an interest in your dreams means taking an interest in yourself. We should therefore always try to analyse them, not only when we are having problems in our lives. The interpretation process in general allows the dreamer to discover aspects of their personality which they did not even know existed: in other words, dreaming helps you to get to know yourself better. Adherents of this approach claim that it allows you to open the door to an objective reality, the profound part of yourself stripped of all conditioning, fear and guilt. Could there be something to this, or is it just an unrealistic fantasy? That is for you to decide.

---

1. This quotation has been translated by 50Minutes.com.

SOME TIPS TO DECIPHER YOUR DREAMS

Remembering your dreams

Dream analysis is not something that can be made up as you go along. Nonetheless, there are methods to help you interpret your dreams alone, without resorting to psycho-therapy. However, before you try any of these, the first thing you need to do is remember your dreams. How can you go about this?

- The quality of our sleep also influences our dreams. It is therefore essential to avoid heavy dinners and all kinds of stimulants before you begin to unwind. You should also make sure to turn off your television or computer at least one hour before you go to bed. Another thing to avoid is intensive exercise late at night. Finally, your room should ideally be both completely silent and dark.
- It is important to be aware of the fact that you are going to dream and you are going to do your best to remember your dreams. Many experts agree that the best way to not forget them is to take an active interest in them. In order to do so, you can try repeating the following mantra: "I am going to dream and I am going to remember my dreams".
- Here is a little ritual to try out: before going to sleep, drink half of a glass of water. Leave the glass beside you on your bedside table. When you wake up, finish your water. This little trick is supposed to help to reactivate your memories.

Since it is more common to remember your dreams at

the end of the night, when your sleep is interrupted more frequently by micro-awakenings, there are memorisation techniques you can test in the morning.

- In *The Everything Dreams Book*, the astrologist Jenni Kosarin recommends setting your alarm 15 to 20 minutes earlier than usual and then, when you wake up, immediately pressing the "snooze" button and going back to sleep again. After two or three times, this technique supposedly helps you to remember your dreams more easily.
- When you come out of a dream, the best thing to do is to remain lying down, with your eyes closed, in order to allow the images to come flowing back to you. If nothing happens, try changing position. You can also think about some important people in your life, which could bring back some elements of the dream.
- Another strategy often recommended by psychologists is to keep a dream diary that you update every morning. Ideally, you should write up everything when you wake up, even if it does not seem to make much sense. The classic questions "who", "what" "where", "when" and "how" can guide you. Your memories will gradually come flooding back to you. This habit will even allow you to remember your dreams more often.
- Recording yourself speaking as soon as you wake up, even with your eyes closed, is another possible method, which has the advantage of requiring less concentration than writing. In a certain sense, this is the moment when we are the closest to our dreams.

Understanding the meaning of your dreams

Have you managed to remember your dreams thanks to some of these good reflexes? It is now time to reflect on them. There is no universal rule for understanding your dreams and dream dictionaries should not be your reference. Moreover, although symbol dictionaries can steer you in the right direction as regards the symbolism of an element in your dream, the dream itself must be interpreted by taking yourself and your personal history into account.

Although there are a number of ways to interpret your dreams, there are still some general tips you can apply to analyse them and uncover their meaning. Begin by carefully going over your notes in your dream journal and asking yourself the right questions.

- What is the general structure of the dream? What does it begin with? How does it develop and how does it end?
- What are the main features? What characters, places, symbols and key images are there?
- What emotions did your dream bring about? Analyse how you felt: for example, were you happy, scared, angry, or powerless?
- What is the link between your dream and your current situation? What does this tell you about your feelings and the obstacles that you are facing?

While thinking of answers to these general questions, do not forget the following advice:

- Be objective and do not invent a plot when there is not

one.

- Do not make things more complicated than they actually are; the meaning is often right under your nose.
- If your dream involves a scene from a film that you watched the night before or some other recent activity, there is no point in looking for further meaning. However, according to some psychotherapists, there is a reason for even the simplest dreams.
- If you are suffering from recurring nightmares, ask yourself if they could be linked to a recent trauma (an assault or a sudden death, for example), in which case you should consult a specialist.
- Pay particular attention to the details; they are often extremely important and should not be overlooked.
- Draw your dream if you feel like it. Drawing supposedly leads to extra details appearing and makes a dream less abstract.

The next thing you should do is reread your notes, using them to visualise and thereby relive your dream. In this way, questions and answers will come to you naturally. Patrick Bertoliatti, a counselling psychologist who specialises in the study of dreams, claims that this sometimes confirms what we already feel, and sometimes gives us unexpected answers.

Two examples of recurring symbols

Although it cannot be denied that symbol dictionaries can only give us general indications, it is also true that there are certain key images which recur in dreams. The first thing to do upon waking up, if you have a symbol dictionary at home, is to start reading and see what it can tell you.

The home is often a central element in our dreams. Several symbolists agree that it represents what is going on inside us. For Freud, this concerns the body, while Jung claims that it is actually a question of the soul. It is essential to examine the rooms of the house we dream about: the kitchen symbolises psychological transformation and evolution, because it is the place where we make ingredients into meals; the bedroom represents our sentimental and sexual lives; and the lift is the representation of spiritual elevation par excellence and takes us to different levels of our psyche.

On another note, dreaming about losing your teeth is also very common. Although this was seen in Antiquity as a bad omen, such as losing someone close to you, this symbol has now taken on a much broader meaning. This kind of dream could therefore represent a loss of vigour or vitality.

Some examples of interpretations

Independently of recurring symbols, the content of dreams is strongly linked to the dreamer's personal experiences. With this in mind, the people who have given us the following testimonies have tried to interpret their dreams by themselves.

Sarah was having a recurring nightmare that she could not understand, because there were certain details which escaped her. After making several attempts to establish a link with her personal situation, she became aware that she was suffering from a certain malaise which she had never realised.

> "I had been haunted by the same nightmare for several nights. I live on the second floor of a small apartment block and so I tend to take the lift. In my dream, I was being chased by a masked stranger, and I tried to escape up the stairs, taking them two at a time. I never stopped running, but no matter how many stairs I rushed up, I couldn't get any further than the second floor. In the end, I would stumble and the person would catch up with me. They would begin to approach me, a knife in one hand and a detective novel in the other. I would then realise that the stranger in question was a woman – my mother – and that she was about to murder me, like what happens in the book. That's when I would wake up. When I began to think about my dream in relation to my real-life situation, I realised that it was a representation of my fear of the future. I had the feeling that I wasn't going anywhere in life, of not growing up and being trapped as a teenager, because I still lived with my mother. My nightmare hasn't come back since." (Sarah, 27)

As for Clara, her dream would force her to relive a recent experience mixed with elements from her past. The completely ordinary event of the day before must have stirred up deep fears which went back to her childhood.

> "I recently dreamed that I met a young woman on the landing of the building where I lived when I was a child. I had no idea who she was. She must have thought I was staring at her, because she shouted angrily at me, 'What are you looking at?' At that moment, I felt really uncomfortable, all the more so since I didn't think I had looked at her funny. It was only when I woke up that I released that she was actually the waitress from the restaurant the day before. She had

made a mistake in my bill, and it had really annoyed me. I
think I used my dream to let out the anger I had held back in
the restaurant." (Clara, 29)

Marine, on the other hand, had a precognitive dream.
According to several psychoanalysts, this type of dream
not only exists, but also proves that our subconscious has a
far greater ability to predict the future than we do when we
are awake. Dr Jean-Michel Crabbé, the author of *Sommeil et
rêves* ("Sleep and Dreams"), observes that the unconscious,
for reasons which have never been understood, sometimes
manages to connect two people who are physically separate
from one another but emotionally close. This seems to be
the case for Marine:

"Several years ago, while I was living away from home
at university, I woke up with a start one night after a very
distressing, extremely clear dream, although it wasn't quite
a nightmare. I was in a cemetery; I had gone there alone,
without knowing why. A burial was taking place not far
from me. I heard a rather vague conversation between two
women about losing a loved one. Then, suddenly, I saw my
grandmother approach me. Her icy blue eyes were fixed on
me intensely. She didn't say a word, and the expression on
her face was unreadable. It was at that moment that I woke
up with a knot in my stomach, as if her gaze had pierced my
very soul. Two days later, the very day I was going home to
visit a friend, my grandmother passed away. She was old, but
she wasn't ill. It was very unexpected; I didn't even have the
time to go see her. Suddenly, my dream flashed before my
eyes." (Marine, 30)

IN CONCLUSION

No matter whether you analyse them on your own or under the guidance of a psychoanalysist, your dreams will allow you to learn more about your aspirations and your mental blocks, and may even help you to get over them. This increase in clarity will help you, for example, to change certain aspects of your behaviour, to turn the page after a particular event or to face an obstacle with more confidence. Depending on your personality and what you want, you could also discuss it with a friend, a step which is highly recommended by certain psychologists. The geekiest among you might be interested to know that a new trend has recently appeared on the internet: applications and websites for sharing your dreams. That being said, modern technology cannot replace your own work or that of a specialist, because you are the only ones who can decipher your dreams and move beyond the stage of simply sharing them.

FAQS

DOES EVERYONE DREAM?

Yes, everyone dreams, as long as they have not taken any particular types of medication. Infants appear to dream much more than adults. Some people in comas even mention having had dreams when they wake up. However, it has never been scientifically proven that it is possible to dream while in a coma. Aside from humans, REM sleep can also be observed in other mammals and in birds. If we suppose that this type of sleep is accompanied by dreams, then we can therefore affirm that all of these animals dream like us.

DO WE CONSTANTLY DREAM WHEN WE ARE ASLEEP?

Although it is true that, after experiments in the 1950s, the scientific community has long defended a direct correlation between REM sleep, which happens roughly every 90 minutes, and the occurrence of dreams, this theory has been questioned since the start of the 21st century. Today, neuroscientists are no longer so sure about the exact periods of sleep during which we dream. It is therefore difficult to confirm not only whether or not we dream constantly throughout the whole night, but also the precise moment when it happens.

WHAT IS THE POINT OF DREAMS?

The answer to this question differs depending on who you ask. A sleep doctor will tell you that analysing dreams is only useful for diagnosing potential sleep problems, while a psychoanalysist will argue that, on the contrary, they have far more use than just that. Psychoanalysists who analyse dreams are convinced that the dream world contains completely objective information about an individual, which is useful not only in cases of psychological pain, but also – in a more general sense – for anyone who would like to get to know themselves a little better.

WHY DO I NOT ALWAYS REMEMBER MY DREAMS?

We know that 90% of our dreams are erased from our memory the moment we wake up. In order to avoid this, our brain needs time to transfer a dream to our conscious memory. This is only possible through micro-awakenings, which take place while we sleep. Certain experiments carried out by neuroscientists have shown that individuals with longer micro-awakenings – lasting around two minutes – remember the content of their dreams better. However, neuroscience has not yet managed to prove that remembering your dreams increases your quality of life. Moreover, there are some people who say that they never remember their dreams and get along just fine.

WHAT ARE PRECOGNITIVE DREAMS? DO THEY REALLY EXIST?

Carl Gustav Jung, as well as many other psychiatrists, has studied the existence of precognitive dreams. In his opinion, this type of dream really does exist and proves the superior ability of the unconscious to anticipate changes that are taking place in reality, but which escape the grasp of your conscious self.

CAN DREAMS INFLUENCE MY EVERYDAY LIFE?

If you remember them, then yes, of course. A psychoanalyst will tell you that analysing your dreams and paying attention to their message will have a positive impact on your daily life. However, the interpretation of dreams is, in itself, not necessary to be happy. In fact, you can completely ignore your dreams with no effect on your quality of life. The benefits of finding out more, for those who sleep and dream normally, are still disputed.

However, in extreme cases, certain particularly frightening recurring nightmares can ruin the days and nights of some people. These dreams are not to be taken lightly, and they can cause so much suffering that there is no choice but to consult a psychoanalysist or a sleep doctor. In particular, these nocturnal disturbances could indicate sleep problems or other illnesses that a somnologist will be able to identify.

HOW CAN I INTERPRET MY DREAMS BY MYSELF?

There is no universal rule to interpret what your dreams mean, and although dictionaries of symbols can point you in the right direction as regards the symbolism of a certain element, the interpretation of your dreams must be personal and linked to your own experiences.

The first thing to do is to make sure that you have satisfied all the conditions for a good night's sleep: eat a light dinner, avoid any stimulants and, above all, relax! Write down your dreams in a notebook when you wake up, or record your account of them on your phone. Ask yourself questions about what you have written down or recorded: what are the key elements, what emotions did you feel? You can then move on to the interpretive phase: what links can I make with my current situation? What information can I take from my dreams as regards my current situation and my weaknesses?

We want to hear from you!
Leave a comment on your online library
and share your favourite books on social media!

FURTHER READING

BIBLIOGRAPHY

- Aimelet, A. (2016) Je ne me souviens jamais de mes rêves. *Psychologies.com*. [Online]. [Accessed 9 June 2017]. Available from: <http://www.psychologies.com/Therapies/Psychanalyse/Reves/Articles-et-Dossiers/Je-ne-me-souviens-jamais-de-mes-reves >
- Alberganti, M. (2014) Faut-il et peut-on se débarrasser des cauchemars ? *Science publique*. France Culture.
- Colin, D. (2011) *L'interprétation des rêves pour les nuls*. Paris: First Éditions.
- Crabbé, J-M. (2015) Le sommeil paradoxal : la neuro-psychologie étonnante du rêve. *Sitemed*. [Online]. [Accessed 9 June 2017]. Available from: <http://www.sitemed.fr/reves/3paradox.htm>
- Crabbé, J-M. (2003) *Sommeil et rêves*. Paris: Ellébore.
- Daco, P. (2007) *L'interprétation des rêves*. Paris: Marabout.
- Eichenlaub, J-B., Bertrand, O., Morlet, D. and Ruby, P. (2013) Brain Reactivity Differentiates Subjects with High and Low Dream Recall Frequencies During Both Sleep and Wakefulness. *Cerebral Cortex*. [Online]. [Accessed 9 June 2017]. Available from: <https://academic.oup.com/cercor/article/24/5/1206/387425/Brain-Reactivity-Differentiates-Subjects-with-High>
- Garteiser, M. (2013) Que révèlent vos rêves et vos cauchemars ? *E-santé*. [Online]. [Accessed 9 June 2017]. Available from: <http://www.e-sante.be/que-revelent-vos-reves-ou-vos-cauchemars/

actualite/1185>

- Inserm vidéos. (2014) Pourquoi le cerveau se souvient-il de nos rêves ? *Youtube*. [Online]. [Accessed 9 June 2017]. Available from: <https://www.youtube.com/watch?v=b94oprdrWe4>
- Kosarin, J. (2008) *Tout sur les rêves*. Varennes: Ada Éditions.
- Lambert, B. (2014) Est-ce que c'est grave de ne pas se souvenir de ses rêves ? *Atlantico*. [Online]. [Accessed 9 June 2017]. Available from: <http://www.atlantico.fr/rdv/atlanti-question-lundi/est-que-cest-grave-ne-pas-se-souvenir-reves-perrine-ruby-1815258.html>
- Mascret, D. (2015) Comment le cerveau se souvient-il de certains rêves ? *Le Figaro*. [Online]. [Accessed 9 June 2017]. Available from: <http://sante.lefigaro.fr/actualite/2015/04/09/23607-comment-cerveau-se-souvient-il-certains-reves>
- Mazelin Salvi, F. (2015) 5 étapes pour interpréter vos rêves. *Psychologies magazine*, 348.
- Science et Vie Junior. (2013) *Les rêves et le sommeil*. Special issue 98.
- Taubes, I. (2015) Comprendre cet "autre" qui vit en vous. *Psychologies magazine*, 348.

ADDITIONAL SOURCES

- Friedman, J. (2015) *The Dream Workbook: A Practical Guide to Understanding Your Dreams and Having them Work for You*. CreateSpace Independent Publishing Platform.
- Tenzin-Dolma, L. (2006) *Understanding Your Dreams:*

A-Z of Dream Explanations and Your Own Dream Diary.
Northamptonshire: Igloo Books Ltd.

IMPROVE YOUR GENERAL KNOWLEDGE

IN A BLINK OF AN EYE !

www.50minutes.com

www.50minutes.com

Ebook EAN: 9782806299918

Paperback EAN: 9782806299949

Legal Deposit: D/2017/12603/408

Cover: © Primento

Digital conception by Primento, the digital partner of publishers.

Made in the USA
Monee, IL
07 July 2026

56545325R10022